Red Summer Race Riot Chicago 1919

Eyewitnesses John Harris and Ida B. Wells

Narrated By Acie Cargill

Formatted - Brenda Van Niekerk

brenda@triomarketers.com

Website Design - Brenda Van Niekerk

http://triomarketers.com

Synopsis

1919 was a year of racial turmoil in America. The Great Migration from the South to Northern Cities was taking place Also hundreds of thousands of African American soldiers were returning home from World War I where they had fought for freedom and were willing to stand up for it in America. Another factor was a black and white silent film Birth of a Nation was released and glorified the Ku Klux Klan and racial fighting and it was very popular and was even shown at the White House. Two hundred black sharecroppers had been murdered in Arkansas and there were hundreds of lynchings across the country.

This account is based on two eyewitness reports by John Harris and Ida B. Wells. They were there and saw what was going on in Chicago and how it got started. It was a terrible year in America and this is just one of the trouble spots. There was violence in many cities and towns and in the country. Hopefully it will never happen again.

About the Author

Acie Cargill is a poet, a songwriter, and a prose writer. He studied poetry with USA Poet Laureate Mark Strand and Illinois Poet Laureate Gwendolyn Brooks. He studied novel writing with Thomas Berger, who wrote Little Big Man (that Arthur Penn made into a movie with Dustin Hoffman in the lead role). Cargill also studied journalism with instructor Jean Daily. His work is a synthesis of all these styles.

He is a member of American Mensa and formerly Edited the Mensa Journal of Poetry. He also is a member of the Grammy Association, and The US Quill and Scroll Society.

Cargill is a vegetarian, a former holistic physician, a musical performer on a variety of instruments, an environmental activist, a lecturer, medical reviewer, a lover, and a seer.

Website

http://aciecargill.com

Contact

aciecargill@gmail.com

Other Books Written by the Author:

Puerto Rico

Aberrations

Chronicles

Terrorism

Modern Love

Ends and odds

Illiana: The Border Area Between Illinois and Indiana

Pullman

Che and Fidel - A Reading Play of the Cuban Revolution

Celia Sanchez - A Play of the Cuban Revolution

Paschke - A Play

Gwendolyn Brooks: A Play

Rasputin - A Play

Nietzsche - A Play

Bob Dylan, The Early Years - A Musical Play

Michael Jackson - A Play

Einstein - A Biographical Play

El Chapo - A Play In 3 Acts

Raisins and Roaches - A Three Month Diary of a Crack Addict

Susan B. Anthony - A Biographical Play

Kankakee

Harriet Tubman - A Biographical Play

Tesla - A Biographical Play

Vegan Saint - A Play in 3 Acts

Martin Luther King, Jr - A Play

Great Migration: A Play in 3 Acts

George Pullman - A Play in Three Acts

Frederick Douglass - A Biographical Play

Freud - A Biographical Play in 3 Acts

The Underground Railroad - An Educational Play

Payton, Jordan, Ali - A Biographical Play

Mr. Nobody - A Play

The Kid From Left Field - A Play

Puerto Rico, A Dream of Independence - A Play in 3 Acts

Crack Madness - A Monologue Play

Johnny Appleseed - A Family Play

Dr. Jekll and Mr. Hyde - A Modernized Play

Obama - Obama - A Play In 3 Acts

Will Rogers - A Biographical Monologue

Merle Haggard - A Biographical Monologue

Mother Teresa - A Biographical Monologue

Gwendolyn Brooks - A Biographical Monologue

Love Life of Susan B. Anthony - A Monologue Play

Sojourner Truth - A Biographical Monologue plus Narrator

Harriet Tubman and The Underground Railroad - A Play

Helen Keller, Words and Wisdom - A Biographical Play

Eugene Debs and the 1894 Pullman Strike - A Play

The Rising - A Play

Walt Disney - A Biographical One Act Play

The Experiments of Dr. Victor Frankenstein - A Play - Based on the novel by Mary Shelley

Karl Marx - A One Act Play

Martin Luther at The Diet of Worms - A One Act Play

Martin Luther King: Monologue and Narrator Play

Frederick Douglass - Monologue and Narrator Play

Kaepernick - A One Act Play

Settling South Holland - A Play In 2 Acts

Kaepernick - A Full-Length Play

My Son Died From An Overdose - A Play

Overdose - A One Act Play

Always a Marine First

Erotic Muslim Polygamy

George Dolton's Bridge to Freedom Underground Railroad - A One-Act Play

Greta Thunberg - A One-Act Play About Climate Change

A Brief History of the Philippines

Goat With No Horns - Voodoo Cannibals in Haiti

Johnny Cash - Monologue Play

Muhammad Words Of Wisdom

Jesus Words Of Wisdom

Bob Hope - Biographical Monologue

The Cargills of Graves County, Ky

Keith Raniere and the NXIVM Sex Club

Words of Wisdom – Native Americans, Ancient Greeks, Buddha and African-Americans

Words of Wisdom – Mark Twain, Benjamin Franklin, Shakespeare and Solomon

The Trial of Eddie Gallagher, Navy SEAL

Climate Crisis - A Plan to Prevent Future Flooding

Yukio Mishima - Life, Death, Hara Kiri

My "Cuzin Willie" Nelson - A Biographical Monologue

The World's Most Amazing Person, Elon Musk

The Beatles: Early Years - A One-Act Play

What could be more terrifying than a race riot? People killing each other just because of skin color. Burning their homes. Rape, pillage, lynchings, terrorizing each other in every way imaginable. Because of race. What set this terrible chaos off? Before this, the cities were fairly peaceful. The different races lived in neighborhoods near each other and accepted things the way they were. 1917 and 1918 there were some flareups of trouble, but in 1919 there were mass killings and destruction. American cities became full of hatred as never before and it turned to violence.

The term "Red Summer," referred to the bloodshed being spilled in race riots across the country. From April to November in 1919, hundreds of Americans, mostly black, would die, and thousands more were injured. Lynchings and indiscriminate killings. Elaine, Arkansas, saw the most horrifying of all when 237 black sharecroppers were murdered over two days for trying to form a union. In that year there were 78 lynchings and 11 black men burned alive at the stake. What a terrible year for America.

Cultural and economic factors combined in 1919 to create conditions ripe for the violence. D.W. Griffith's 1915 "Birth of a Nation", a black and white silent film, screened at the White House and was enthusiastically received by President Wilson. It glorified the Ku Klux Klan as heroes, as saviors of southern white women during Reconstruction after the Civil War and the emancipation of the slaves. The movie was a blockbuster and helped bring about a rebirth of the Klan, which grew from a few thousand members to over 5 million by the 1920s. With the rise of the Klan came a rise in racial hatred.

Meanwhile, in the Great Migration more than a hundred thousand blacks moved from the cotton fields of the South to the factories of the North. Soldiers returning from World War I sought jobs, too. At least 350,000 African-American soldiers had fought in World War I for freedom, but when they returned they found the prejudice and hatred was still going strong in the North and the South.

The Red Summer was a moment when black citizens showed they had had enough, and fought back for their rights. The indignation was captured in a July poem by Harlem Renaissance writer Claude McKay. "If We Must Die" was the Red Summer anthem.

What though before us lies the open grave?

Like men we'll face the murderous, cowardly pack,

Pressed to the wall, dying, but fighting back!

Chicago wasn't the only city besieged by mob violence in the months after World War I.. Between late 1918 and late 1919, the US saw 10 major anti-black riots, and dozens of minor, racially charged clashes.

Many black men and women were killed that year in racial violence. Nobody knows how many. The unofficial death toll was hundreds of people -- the majority of whom were black -- across the country.

For nearly a week in the summer of 1919, Chicago descended into "a certain madness," in the words of the city's leading black newspaper, the *Chicago Defender*. White mobs assaulted virtually any black person they could find on the streets, and blacks engaged in deadly acts of retaliation and self-defense. By the time the violence subsided, 38 men — 23 of them black and 15 white — had been killed and more than 500 people were injured. "Chicago is disgraced and dishonored," the *Chicago Daily Tribune* declared. "Its head is bloodied and bowed, bloodied by crime and bowed in shame. Its reputation is besmirched. It will take a long time to remove the stain."

At the time of the riot, the composition of the city was changing, fueling tensions. From 1910 to 1920, Chicago's black population had grown from about 44,000 to nearly 110,000 — still just 4 percent of the city's 2.7 million residents — as Southern blacks moved north to flee Jim Crow laws. Previously, most black Chicagoans lived in an area called the Black Belt, from 22nd Street (now Cermak Road) south to 39th Street (now Pershing Road) and from Wentworth Avenue east to State Street. Now they were starting to move into bordering neighborhoods like Hyde Park and Kenwood..

A noted journalist, Ida B. Wells said in 1919 in the Chicago Tribune after white gangs had attacked black citizens. "It looks very much like Chicago is trying to rival the South in its race hatred against the Negro. Will no action be taken to prevent these lawbreakers until further disaster has occurred?"

Here is an eyewitness account of what started the trouble from 15 year old John Harris. "It was the hottest weekend of the year, with temperatures hitting 95. Chicagoans crowded the beaches."

"I went to the 25th Street beach. This is where most of the Negroes went. Now, on 29th Street, the white people formed the little beach right behind Michael Reese Hospital. The funny thing is, I didn't question it. If you don't want to be bothered with me, I don't want to be bothered with you. They had their little beach. And they were welcome to come over to ours anytime they wished — and they did, when they wanted some seclusion. We were not allowed over there, because there was always a fight. Nothing I wanted was over there anyway. So we had a colored lifeguard and a colored policeman to the 25th Street beach."

"We would put in our little raft. It was a nice size — about 14 by 9 feet. Oh, we were pushing this raft in the water, not getting too far. None of us were accomplished swimmers, but we could dive underwater and come up. We would push the raft and swim, kick, dive, and play around. As long as the raft was there, we were safe.'

"The trouble started when two Negro couples appeared on what is called the "white section" of the improvised 29th Street beach and demanded the right to enter the water there. When refused, according to whites, they became abusive and threatened to return soon with a crowd of their friends and "clean up the place." It was not long before the Negroes were back, coming from the north with others of their race. Then began a series of attacks and retreats, counterattacks, and stone throwing. Women and children who could not escape hid behind debris and rocks. The stone throwing continued, first one side gaining the advantage, then the other."

"Around 3 or 4 p.m., we pushed the raft southeast, passing a breakwater that jutted into the lake at 26th Street and nearing the white area. One of the boys was Eugene Williams, a black 17-year-old Georgia native who worked as a grocery porter."

"This white fellow was walking along the breakwater. It had to be between 75 and 100 feet from us. We were watching him. He'd take a rock and throw it, and we would duck. As long as we could see him, he never could hit us — because, after all, a guy throwing that far is not a likely shot. One fellow would say, "Look out, here comes one," and we would duck. It was just like a little game. This went on for a long time.".

"Eugene had just come up and went to dive again when somebody averted his attention. And just as he turned his head, this fellow threw a rock and it struck him on the right side of his forehead. I had just come up, and I could see something was wrong. He didn't dive — he just sort of relaxed. I went under with him and saw the blood from his head. He grabbed my right ankle. And hell, I got scared. I shook him off. We were in about 15 feet of water at the time, and I had gone down about 10 feet with him. You could see the blood coming up."

"Let's get the lifeguard." So I got a breath and swam underwater till I got to the island, then I got up and ran over to the beach, which is a good block away. I told the head lifeguard — Butch, they called him — and he blew a whistle and sent a boat around. He ran along with me and dove in and went to the raft. The boys were still on it. They were panic-stricken, but they kept their eye on this fellow who threw the rocks. This colored cop walked along the shore with me. We pointed the fellow out. He was nervous."

"So the colored cop went to arrest him, and the white cop would not let him arrest him. There was a big argument between the two policemen. We ran back to the 25th Street beach and told the colored people. In the meantime, the lifeguard had gotten the boy's body, and naturally all the people came over and demanded that they arrest the man. And this is when the fight started. If the police had been on the ball, nothing would have happened, but they started beating people, clubbing them."

Reports of the drowning and of the alleged conduct of the policeman spread out into the neighborhood. A mob of about 1,000 Negroes congregated at 29th Street and Cottage Grove Avenue. Policemen attempting to disperse the mob were assaulted. James Crawford, a Negro, fired a revolver directly into the group of policemen. They retaliated, and Crawford ran. A Negro policeman followed Crawford, attempting to stop him by firing. Crawford was wounded and died two days later on July 29.

Excitement ran high all through the day. Groups of men whose minds were inflamed by rumors of brutal attacks on men, women, and children crowded the public thoroughfares in the South Side district from 27th to 39th Streets, some voicing sinister sentiments, and the remainder making their way home to grease up the old family revolver.

Added to the already irritable feeling was the fact that some whites had planned to make a visit to the South Side homes with guns and torches. This message was conveyed to a group of men who were congregated near 36th Street, on State.

Around 4:30 p.m., a 64-year-old fruit merchant named Casimiro Lazzaroni, who'd come to America from Italy in the 1880s, was stabbed to death on State Street, just south of 36th Street. An hour later on the same block, a 31-year-old white Chicago native named Eugene Temple was stabbed to death as he walked out of the laundry he owned. Authorities said the assailants in both slayings were black.

Ida B. Well wrote "Free Chicago stands today humble before the world. She has shown that with all her resources, her splendid police force, her military reserve, her culture, and her civilization, she is weak and helpless before the mob. Notwithstanding our boasted democracy, lynch law is king."

"Lawless mobs roam our streets. They kill inoffensive citizens and no notice is taken. They are Negroes — they are only Negroes — and it doesn't matter. Houses have been bombed and lives taken in our glorious, free city, but it is only a few Negroes. They have had the nerve to move into white neighborhoods. It serves them right. Why should Chicago bother to make democracy safe for Negroes?"

"Race prejudice is as old as the world and so it is dismissed with a wave of the hand. A Negro wishes to bathe in the lake on a hot day as the rest of our cosmopolitan population. He is hit with a brick while in the water and drowned to make sport for the heathen because he dared come into the water where they are. Who cares? He is only a Negro, and Negroes have no rights that whites are bound to respect."

"Adding to the chaos, the third day began with streetcar employees going on strike. As a result, more people than usual walked the streets that morning. The riot violence spread into the Loop, where white mobs killed two black men. I saw some really vicious-looking white hoodlums, mostly young, unkempt — distinctly different from the mass of people who were walking to work."

"At the end of the day I was driven home in government trucks, which were protected by armed guards. During our ride home we passed many areas where there were roaming mobs of white hoodlums — we could not help but feel how much we depended on these guards and what would be our fate if the guards did not perform their duty."

"I felt a certain sense of helplessness and that I did not feel that the city police were in any way handling the situation and, quite the opposite, the police frequently not only joined the mobs but stood by and saw people beaten and killed without making any effort at all to apprehend the persons responsible. One of my neighbors had been very badly beaten the night before by a group while the police looked on."

"Hundreds of desperate or rough-looking white men could be observed rushing west from Racine Avenue and from other points to Ada and Loomis Streets. When we beheld a mob of almost 4,000 men crowding around the corners of those streets, that they fully intended to set fire to the homes of all the colored people in that district that very night and then shoot the negro residents down like rats or mad dogs, while they were fleeing for their lives. They were just foaming to get each other. The Negroes were yelling, 'Let 'em come!' And the whites were yelling, 'We're coming!'"

"The rioting was eventually brought under control when the Governor of Illinois, Frank Lowden, sent the Illinois national Guard to Chicago, fully armed and ready to fight and the rioters and mobs decided to stay home instead of fighting the troops."

The 15 white fatalities included five men who were apparently killed as they were committing acts of violence. Police bullets killed at least five — and possibly as many as eight — of the 23 black victims, but no officers faced any criminal charges. The racial discrepancy in the cases being brought before it was not lost on the all-white grand jury. "It is the opinion of this jury that the colored people suffered more at the hands of the white hoodlums than the white people suffered at the hands of the black hoodlums," it said in a statement. "Notwithstanding this fact, the cases presented to this jury against the blacks far outnumber those against the white. The Negro is silent, but he is thinking. He cannot be expected to remain patient forever under these continued attacks."

The Cook County state's attorney, Maclay Hoyne, later said: "There is no doubt that a great many police officers were grossly unfair in making arrests. They shut their eyes to offenses committed by white men while they were very vigorous in getting all the colored men they could get."

"Governor Lowden created the Chicago Commission on Race Relations and appointed 12 men — six white and six black — to find solutions to racial tension. For his part, the governor believed there should be a "tacit understanding" of separate residential areas, beaches, and parks for blacks and whites, leading some to believe that the Governor would encourage the continuation of segregation"

Made in the USA
Middletown, DE
07 September 2021